Original title:
In the Palm of Paradise

Copyright © 2025 Creative Arts Management OÜ
All rights reserved.

Author: Alexander Thornton
ISBN HARDBACK: 978-1-80581-565-5
ISBN PAPERBACK: 978-1-80581-092-6
ISBN EBOOK: 978-1-80581-565-5

Twilight's Kiss on Blissful Shores

Seagulls gossip, feathers ruffled,
A crab in pants, all too muffled.
The waves break into bubbly jest,
As seaweed dances in a fest.

Flip-flops slapped, a runaway shoe,
Turtles snicker, watching the crew.
A cocktail spills with lemonade cheer,
Splashing the sun, the giggles draw near.

Wanderlust in the Shade of Silence

Under the tree, a squirrel sings,
Chasing acorns and all such things.
A picnic spread, ants on parade,
The sandwich thief already displayed.

A napkin flies, a gust so bold,
As the lemonade turns to cold gold.
With sunglasses on, the cat's a star,
In daydreams lost, we've come so far.

A Tapestry Woven in Whispered Dreams

Clouds wear pajamas, fluffy and bright,
As stars plan pranks to light up the night.
Up above, owls spin tales anew,
While fireflies dance, a glowing crew.

A blanket fort, with snacks piled high,
We argue if marshmallows could fly.
The moon winks down, a quirky knight,
Unraveling jokes hidden from sight.

Traces of Illumined Dawn

Sunrise giggles through breakfast toast,
A pancake flips, a chef's proud boast.
The coffee's bold, then takes a leap,
As sleepy heads begin to peep.

A rooster fumbles, trying to crow,
But all he does is cluck and glow.
With laughter rising, the day takes flight,
In the morning's glow, everything's just right.

Eternal Blooms and Starlit Paths

In a garden where giggles grow,
The flowers dance with a humorous glow.
Bees wear hats and the daisies wink,
While tomatoes giggle as they start to sink.

Nightfall brings stars dressed in jest,
They twinkle like jokes that never rest.
The moon leans close to eavesdrop a pun,
While rabbits are plotting their next funny run.

Serenity within the Green Embrace

A turtle in slippers strolls with flair,
Chasing a rabbit who just doesn't care.
Frogs in bow ties croak a sweet tune,
While veggies debate who'll dance at noon.

Lush leaves whisper with cheeky delight,
As crickets provide tunes for the night.
Squirrels squirrel away all the snacks,
While laughing with friends, they plot their tracks.

Where the Wildflowers Whisper

Wildflowers chuckle beneath the sun,
Bouncing and bobbing, just having fun.
Bees hold meetings to vote on the bloom,
While blossoms joke of a broom in full plume.

A butterfly slips on a petal or two,
Gliding through giggles like nothing is new.
Grasshoppers leap with a joke on their lips,
Mocking the wind as they sway on their trips.

A Symphony of Sun and Shade

In shadows where sunshine plays hide and seek,
The blooms discuss who will be the next freak.
A sunflower spins tales of a funny fate,
While dusk tips its hat, never showing late.

Music from leaves plays tricks on the ear,
While fireflies dance, spreading bold cheer.
Nature's comedians never cease to amaze,
Life's little laughter keeps brightening the days.

The Unfurling of Daydreams

In a land where socks can dance,
And cats wear hats by chance,
We sip on lemonade so bright,
Whilst chasing dreams till the night.

A duck quacks Shakespeare on a bench,
While fish play chess, oh what a wrench!
Clouds try stand-up, but they just float,
As sunlight plays its golden note.

The moon serves coffee, what a treat,
With cookies shaped like little feet.
Giraffes wear ties and sing a tune,
In the wild waltz beneath the moon.

So laugh along this silly spree,
In a world where we can just be!
For in this humor, we're all afloat,
With daydreams unbound, we'll learn to gloat.

Lighthouses of Peace through Verdant Ages

Amid the trees where squirrels gossip,
A turtle runs a flower shop.
His carrots are the finest gems,
While bees sing songs of joy for them.

A parrot plays the saxophone,
As frogs create a joyful zone.
With hats askew and laughter loud,
The woods dance proudly, unbowed.

Each leaf a dancer in the breeze,
Whimsical tales from ancient trees.
The birthdays last for birds in flight,
As starlit dreams embrace the night.

A lizard juggles, what a show!
With endless fun where worries go.
Peaceful lighthouses guide the way,
In vivid greens we choose to play.

Whimsies Underneath Fragrant Boughs

Underneath the boughs so sweet,
A gnome makes pies with tiny feet.
Mice in jackets sip on tea,
While flowers giggle, oh so free!

Raccoons play cards with witty flair,
Laughing loudly without a care.
The daisies wear their Sunday best,
As butterflies take flight, no rest.

The jokes are fresh like morning dew,
As naughty elves now play peek-a-boo.
With fruit hats on, the fun won't cease,
In fragrant world, we find our peace.

So join this troupe of merry sprites,
Where whimsy sparkles and delights.
Adventures bloom like flowers bright,
As joy ignites the starry night.

Garden of Whispers

In the garden, gnomes conspire,
Telling secrets by the fire.
Flowers giggle, bees do dance,
Squirrels plotting their romance.

A cabbage dressed in velvet coat,
Believes he's quite the handsome boat.
Rabbits snicker as they hop,
Wishing all their worries stop.

Echoes of Eden

A parrot sings in high-pitched tones,
Making friends with garden stones.
Apples roll, they play tag near,
They'd win the race if they'd not steer.

The tiny ants parade with pride,
In line they march, a grand joyride.
A snail thinks he is quite the king,
While daisies lace the air with spring.

Secrets Beneath the Canopy

Underneath the leafy cloak,
A frog chats with a talking oak.
They share puns, and giggles swell,
As whispers rise, they cast a spell.

A squirrel claims he stole the show,
With acorn jokes, he's quite the pro.
The shadows play their mischief games,
While owls roll eyes at all the claims.

Nestled in Nature's Cradle

In a nest, a chick did brag,
About his worm-filled snacky bag.
His mom just shook her feathered head,
"Eat your greens," she gently said.

Butterflies wear silly hats,
Chasing moths, they're acrobats.
Laughter bubbles, sunbeams shine,
In this cradle, life's divine.

Twilight's Embrace in the Grove

As nightfall creeps, the crickets sing,
A raccoon dons a crown, he's the king.
Fireflies dance, a shimmering show,
While bushes whisper secrets we don't know.

A squirrel juggles acorns in flight,
While owls hoot jokes, oh what a sight!
The moon looks on, a giggling friend,
In this crazy world, the fun won't end.

Melody of the Midnight Bloom

Flowers hum tunes when the stars are bright,
Petals twirl in rhythm, oh what a sight!
The bees wear hats, buzzing in style,
While a butterfly struts with flair and guile.

Moths flit around, a disco ball's glow,
Sharing their dances, putting on a show.
Nature's serenade, a sweet, silly ballet,
As laughter echoes through the night's display.

The Enchanted Glade Awaits

In a secret spot where the wild things play,
A fox in pajamas has come out to stay.
Bunnies wear sneakers, hopping with glee,
While ferns gossip quietly under a tree.

The breeze makes whispers with silly intent,
Tickling the leaves, oh how they lament!
Branches sway gently, can't help but tease,
Who knew the woods held such wild pranks, please?

Ribbons of Light and Laughter

With ribbons of glow, the night comes alive,
A glowing snail brigade takes a dive.
Laughter erupts as shadows take flight,
Chasing their tails in the soft moonlight.

Silly old trees start doing a jig,
As owls throw a party, oh so big!
With cupcakes for critters and punch for the fun,
This lively affair has only begun.

The Promise of Lucrative Storms

When it rains, the money grows,
And so do all our silly woes.
Umbrellas upside down in flight,
We chase coins till it's out of sight.

Puddles bounce like stress-free snaps,
Collecting dreams and silly naps.
Each wet shoe leads us on a chase,
While ducks laugh, splashing in our face.

We sell umbrellas with no shame,
A stormy business—what a game!
Raindrops dancing on our heads,
Making fortunes out of dreads.

So here's to storms, both wild and calm,
Where laughter's found, instead of qualm.
In every cloud, there's silver's gleam,
When fortune smiles, it's not just a dream.

Colors of a Thousand Hues

The paint is spilled, oh what a sight,
A rainbow vomits day and night.
We slip and slide on colors bright,
Like clowns in dreams, oh what a fright!

Our faces splattered like a canvas,
Each brushstroke yet another madness.
We laugh until our bellies ache,
Fun's the ultimate mistake we make.

Purple skies and yellow grass,
A world, absurd as it will pass.
With every splash, our laughter grows,
In this place where chaos flows.

So join the chaos, splash around,
In every color, joy is found.
With laughter painting every view,
We find our fun in shades anew.

Meditations on Establishing Eden

We plant our seeds in silly pots,
Naming each with ridiculous thoughts.
Are these flowers or giant weeds?
Let's hope they serve our hungry needs!

Garden gnomes with mischief in their eyes,
Whispering secrets, plotting lies.
"Plant pizza trees!" they shout with glee,
Funny how just plants can't agree.

We sit amongst the chaos wild,
Napping under skies so mild.
"Who left the door wide open?" we ask,
As squirrels raid our picnic flask.

Yet in the midst of laughter sweet,
We find life's meaning, oh so neat.
With every bloom, our antics spread,
In this garden of joy, we tread.

Gentle Rhythms of the Drowsy Afternoon

Naps are art in the afternoon,
Pillow fights with a cartoon tune.
Sipping tea with sleepy eyes,
Lost in daydreams, oh how time flies!

The clock mocks us, its hands a tease,
Yet we lounge with effortless ease.
Bumbling through a haze of fun,
This lazy game's never quite done.

Cats yawn wide with fluffy grace,
As we drift in this cozy space.
Who needs to rush? There's nothing to do,
When afternoon's light tickles you.

So laugh between the sleepy sighs,
Chasing butterflies and lazy flies.
In gentle rhythms, joy does bloom,
In drowsy hours, we find our room.

The Art of Serendipity

A squirrel in a top hat,
Dances on a rumor,
While chips of chocolate rain,
Fall like confetti in humor.

A dog barks at the moon,
Confused by its whisker glow,
He chases his own tail,
Amidst giggles and woe.

A cat strums the ukulele,
With style and flair divine,
It meows a tune quite dandy,
That makes the heart align.

So if you trip on a banana,
Embrace the silly slip,
For life's a comedy show,
And laughter's the best trip.

Finding Warmth in Violet Shadows

A turtle wears some shades,
Sipping tea with glee,
In a patch of sunlight,
Where it's just him and me.

Tickling the daisies,
With a butterfly's joke,
They burst into laughter,
As a sleepy sheep yoke.

An owl in a bright tie,
Checks the time with a wink,
His glasses fall off quickly,
As he starts to rethink.

Underneath the violet,
Grin and twirl with delight,
Each giggle a reminder,
That shadows can be bright.

Kaleidoscope of a Dreamscape

A giraffe in a bowtie,
Tries to play the flute,
But gives up for a banana,
And starts a dance dispute.

Clouds shaped like jellybeans,
Float across the blue,
While rainbows tie their laces,
In a cosmic hula-hoo.

A fish in a tuxedo,
Shoots for the marching band,
When splashing out a tempo,
It becomes a wavy strand.

In this dreamscape of giggles,
Colors swirl and bloom,
With every twist and turn,
We banish all the gloom.

Serenity Wrapped in Bloom

A vase of laughing daisies,
Hats on each little head,
They gossip about the breeze,
And dance before the bed.

Bees wear tiny sneakers,
As they buzz all around,
While flowers start a chorus,
In a joyful, silly sound.

A rabbit with a monocle,
Reads poetry to a snail,
Together they concoct,
The silliest of tales.

Wrapped in nature's humor,
With colors bold and bright,
Serenity is laughter,
In the softest daylight.

The Flourish of an Unseen Realm

A squirrel donned a tiny hat,
In a party of fruit, oh how they sat!
Rabbits danced, while mice played flutes,
An unseen realm of giggles and hoots.

The daisies winked, what a sight!
Whilst butterflies boogied into the night.
A toad sang jazz, with great flair,
In this secret hideaway, without a care.

Fragrant Trails of Echoing Heartbeats

Skunks wore perfume, for a laugh,
While bees buzzed in a comical gaff.
Petunias pranced in pastel hues,
Chasing each other to find some shoes.

A heart beat loud, oh what a tune!
As flowers twirled 'neath the silvery moon.
An echo of giggles, light as a breeze,
In this fragrant land, joy never flees.

The Joys of Multicolored Sunsets

A parrot painted with colors bold,
Joked with a snail, oh tales retold!
As the sun dipped low in a grand display,
They laughed together, come what may.

Balloons floated past in shades so bright,
Chasing shadows in the fading light.
The sky giggled, in oranges and pinks,
While critters gathered, sharing their winks.

Gemstones in the Crevices of Time

A turtle sought out treasures rare,
With a wink and a smile, he'd declare:
'Why rush when jewels are found in cracks?'
He chuckled as he carried his snacks.

Each pebble sparkled, a sight to see,
While frogs croaked loud in harmony.
A giggle echoed through ages past,
In the crevices of time, joy lasts.

Pathways Through Silent Glades

In the forest, squirrels prance,
Trees are swaying, what a dance.
Mushrooms giggle, frogs do sing,
It's a wild and silly thing.

Bamboo whispers, tales untold,
Nuts go tumbling, brave and bold.
A sleepy owl looks quite dazed,
In this place, life's always fazed.

Breezes tease the leaves so sly,
Bugs in costumes passing by.
Lizards bask on warm, bright rocks,
Wearing hats like funny flocks.

Mice in robes, they hold a ball,
Toadstools seating, one and all.
Laughter bubbles like a stream,
In these glades, it's all a dream.

Flight of Fancy at Dusk

Bats take wing, it's quite a sight,
They play tag with the waning light.
Fireflies paint the air with glee,
Dancing like they've had some tea.

A raccoon juggles shiny cans,
Doing tricks while no one stands.
An owl hoots a seasoned rhyme,
As critters mingle, it's showtime.

Breezy winds spread giggles wide,
Night unfolds with winks and pride.
Gossip spreads among the trees,
While crickets play their symphonies.

Stars pop out, the show's not done,
Pandas cheer, they've found the fun.
Underneath a twilight grin,
The world twirls, let the games begin!

Spirits Beneath the Tropical Sky

Monkeys plot with cheeky grins,
Their capers lead to silly wins.
Parrots squawk, they're quite the crows,
Their fashion sense? Well, who knows!

Waves are lapping, shells all dance,
An octopus with pearls, by chance.
Sandcastles groan, they can't compete,
When hermit crabs have quite the beat.

A turtle throws a beachside bash,
With tasty treats and lots of splash.
Seashells gossip, join the fray,
This is just a normal day!

Under palms, the laughter swells,
With every wave, the magic tells.
As the sun dips, night takes the prize,
While spirits twinkle, 'neath the skies.

Pomegranates and Passionfruit

Pomegranates roll, a hearty mess,
Each seed a story, I confess.
Passionfruit laughs with zesty cheer,
A tropic carnival is near.

Juicy jokes, they spill and splash,
Fruit flies buzz, their charm a crash.
Mangoes join with a winking grin,
In this fruity tale, let's begin!

Ripe bananas throw a pie,
In the air, they fly so high.
A veggie dance, it's truly grand,
As carrots twirl hand in hand.

Underneath the leafy shade,
Where laughter blooms, a grand parade.
With every bite, delight's unfurled,
A fruity frolic, joy's sweet world.

Secrets of the Enchanted Depths

Underneath the leafy spread,
A squirrel's ninja skills, I dread.
It steals my sandwich, oh so sly,
With furry paws, it waves goodbye.

A frog leaps far, it makes me cackle,
As deer and rabbits share a tackle.
They gambol in a playful race,
While I just sit and eat my face.

The water's gleam reflects the fun,
Fish tease, thinking they've just won,
But I've got snacks—they can't resist!
Oh, nature's chaos, how I've missed!

With giggles ringing through the trees,
Life dances on a gentle breeze.
A grin upon my sun-kissed cheeks,
In wild unrest, it's joy I seek!

A Paradise Found in Quiet Moments

Quiet naps under the sun,
A chipmunk thinks it's all just fun.
It sits on my head like a hat,
And all I do is laugh at that!

Birds chirp in a silly tune,
They've learned their moves from the moon.
Stamping feet on the old tree bark,
Who knew the woods could throw a lark?

Twirling leaves create a mess,
For my hair today, it's a dress!
The wind just giggles with delight,
As I chase my hat with all my might!

Wish you were here to join the spree,
In youthful jest, we'll dare to be.
Among the whispers, laughter grows,
In quiet joy, the heart bestows!

The Lush Embrace of Nature's Bounty

Mangoes tumbling from the tree,
A snack attack? Oh, let it be!
While bees zoom here and there they dart,
I've swatted, missed, and lost my heart.

The bushes rustle; a game of tag,
Who knew nature could be a rag?
With berries squished beneath my feet,
This crunchy dance is quite the feat!

A parrot squawks, "You've got style!"
It flaps and struts—a vibrant mile.
As I tumble down in mirthful glee,
Nature's bounty shares with me!

With every giggle that I share,
The lushest secrets fill the air.
In every nook, a chuckle sprouts,
Oh, life and laughter—what it's about!

Tides of Tranquility in Lush Landscapes

Waves of green, a playful tease,
They sway and dance with gentle ease.
A raccoon slips, gives me a wink,
As I trip over—oh, what a stink!

Breezes whisper silly tales,
As I hop over fallen trails.
Tickled toes in a stream so cool,
Nature's laughter is the best school!

Sunshine pours like honey sweet,
A dance-off with my own two feet.
While butterflies join in the fun,
Circling round until they're done!

In wild delight, we create a sight,
Nature's stage, oh what a delight!
With every giggle, I shed my cares,
In laughing light, my spirit shares!

Dreaming Among the Blissful Fronds

Beneath the leaves where shadows dance,
A squirrel tries to woo a chance.
He spins and twirls, with acorn flair,
But all the birds just stop and stare.

The lizards gossip, tails a-twitch,
About the critter's daring pitch.
With giggles hiding in the breeze,
They toast to him with leafy teas.

A parrot squawks, a comical scene,
"In love with nuts? What could it mean?"
The wind just laughs, a nimble twist,
And all agree it's hard to miss.

So here we dream, where laughter swirls,
With nature's antics and its whirls.
In fronds so blissful, we take part,
With silly joy, we fill our heart.

Serenade of the Hidden Grove

In the grove where mischief lies,
A raccoon dons a mask of guise.
He steals the snacks from unsuspecting folk,
And leaves behind a trail of smoke.

The owls applaud with goofy hoots,
As he nibbles on our dinner roots.
"Another feast, oh what a find,"
They twirl their heads, both wise and blind.

A frog croaks loud, a brash refrain,
"Your finest meal, turned into gain!"
Together they form quite the show,
In a hidden grove where antics flow.

So gather round, let laughter resound,
For in this grove, joy knows no bound.
With every giggle, the night we'll save,
In the serenade of this silly cave.

Sunlit Sanctuaries of Serenity

Beneath the sun, a pig in shades,
Rolls in the grass, the coolest of trades.
With a wink and grunt, he strikes a pose,
While butterflies dance on his toes.

A goat nearby, a comedian at heart,
Jumps on a rock, calls it art.
He bleats a tune, with flair and fun,
While chasing shadows, he's on the run.

The bees join in, they hum and buzz,
Creating rhythms that simply does.
A party here, filled with delight,
In sunlit sanctuaries, everything's right.

So laugh a little, let worries go,
For in this place, we steal the show.
With humor and joy, we'll light the way,
In sunny alleys, where we play.

The Tranquil Refuge Beneath the Stars

Under the stars, a cat on guard,
Makes fierce faces, though it's quite hard.
A mouse walks by, without a care,
Dances with glee, unaware of the stare.

The moon chuckles, in silver glow,
At this little game of "Who's the pro?"
While crickets chirp a night-time tune,
The cat just dreams of chasing the moon.

Fireflies twirl in a sparkling dress,
As owls hoot softly, in a state of mess.
A raccoon snickers, hiding behind,
This peaceful chaos, so fun and blind.

So gather 'round, let laughter be heard,
In this tranquil refuge, spread the word.
With funny antics, and hearts so free,
We celebrate under this starry spree.

Secrets Sown in the Soil's Heart

A potato found wearing a hat,
He danced with the beets, oh what a spat!
Carrots played chess, quite the game,
Bragging rights went up in flame.

The herbs told jokes, so fresh and minty,
While radishes blushed, feeling quite flinty.
Under the sun, they all conspired,
To grow a garden, slightly admired.

The sunflowers giggled, so tall and bright,
Tickling the clouds, what a silly sight!
A party was brewing beneath the green,
With trowels and laughter, what a scene!

As rain fell gently, they splashed in glee,
Each droplet a tune, pure jubilee.
Secrets they whispered to roots out of sight,
In the soil's heart, where dreams took flight.

An Enclave of Gentle Echoes

In a cozy nook where shadows play,
Squirrels held meetings with nothing to say.
A butterfly grinned at a blushing leaf,
Together they plotted, beyond belief.

Rustling leaves laughed, a soft, silly sound,
While crickets composed tunes, totally unbound.
They formed a band, led by the breeze,
Playing sweet songs to tickle the trees.

Nearby, a frog croaked with gusto and cheer,
His mates jumped along, always near.
In this enclave, no worries did dwell,
Just echoes of laughter, a magical spell.

The world seemed strange and bright all around,
Where whispers of mischief and joy could be found.
In this gentle refuge, with odd friends to greet,
Life was a hum, and oh, what a treat!

Lullabies of the Forgotten Oasis

At dawn, the camels wrapped in dreams,
Shared stories of ponds and sunbeams.
Palm trees swayed to a laugh-filled tune,
While cacti danced under the lazy moon.

A parrot squawked, wearing a crown,
Reciting the gossip of the desert town.
With each silly tale, the sun would rise,
Tickling the sky, oh my, what a surprise!

Turtles in shade took their time to weave,
Lullabies cute, you just wouldn't believe.
In whispers soft, the oasis agreed,
That laughter, not water, was the true need.

So the mirage shimmered with giggles galore,
As creatures convened on the sandy floor.
With hidden delights in the wind's gentle sway,
Their lullabies flourished, come what may.

The Dance of Radiant Petals

In the garden's heart, petals pranced,
A daisy slipped, but the rose just danced.
They twirled and spun in the morning's glow,
Creating a show, oh what a row!

Sunbeams giggled, casting golden light,
While tulips debated whose color was bright.
A daffodil shouted, "I'm the best of all!"
Only to trip on a butterfly's call.

The daisies laughed as the marigolds waved,
They teased the shy violets, sweetly engraved.
With colors that shimmered, they painted a scene,
Where laughter blossomed, fresh and serene.

As bees buzzed close with a rhyming hum,
The party kept rolling, oh so much fun!
In the dance of petals, joy took its stand,
As the garden rejoiced, nature's own band.

Chronicles of Pioneering Hearts

We danced on hills of fluffy clouds,
Sipped lemonade in golden shrouds.
With squirrels as our lively guides,
We laughed as we took wild, bumpy rides.

Our dreams were made of cotton candy,
Bouncing ideas, a bit too dandy.
Each plan we hatched had flaps and wings,
Like chickens thinking they could sing.

To build a fort from beach ball chairs,
Claiming it guarded all our wares.
But as we leaned, it fell apart,
Leaving us all with a soggy start.

Through pranks and giggles, tales we spun,
Even in chaos, we had our fun.
With every twist and zany part,
We found our laughter in the heart.

The Enchantment of Wild Blooms

In a garden where daisies wore hats,
Bees waltzed around like friendly brats.
Tulips giggled, rose bushes swayed,
As sunbeams danced, and shadows played.

We tried to chat with a dandelion,
Who claimed it was quite the wise design.
But all it offered was floating fluff,
Guess that profound wisdom wasn't enough.

A butterfly joined, sipping sweet tea,
Kicked off the party with a winged spree.
Laughter arose from petals so bright,
As flowers joined in, a colorful sight.

With mud pies and giggles, we called it a day,
Nature's embrace in a sprightly ballet.
In blooms we found a quirky charm,
Who knew wild could be so warm?

Reflections in Cool Springs

Down by the water where frogs play leap,
We sat on rocks, not making a peep.
A fish splashed and startled our chat,
We all shrieked... and then fell flat!

The wind tickled our noses and toes,
As we sketched in mud, art no one knows.
A heron laughed and stole our lunch,
Leaving us just a soggy brunch.

Our water dreams led us on a quest,
To build the best boat, we tried our best.
But our sails were made of paper and tape,
And soon enough, we went out of shape.

With splashes loud and giggles galore,
We raced our boats to the nearest shore.
Who knew cool springs could hold such cheer?
In wobbly crafts, adventure was near!

A Serenade of Rich Verdure

In jungles thick with leafy surprise,
Monkeys played tricks and wore funny ties.
Each vine we swung on had a great tale,
Of how we escaped a green, goofy snail.

With wildflowers singing in disarray,
We danced with the lizards, who led us astray.
The bushes whispered secrets of green,
A party of critters, quite the scene!

We tried dressing up in grass capes,
Pretending we were the grandest shapes.
But nature laughed, as we got stuck,
In a thicket where one could try their luck.

With food for thought, and laughter so wide,
In this vibrant realm, we took our ride.
Here the verdure sparkled with glee,
A funny serenade—just you and me!

Beneath the Emerald Canopy

Under the leaves so bright,
A squirrel forgot his flight.
He chased a butterfly, oh dear,
Now he's stuck up here in fear.

The parrot's singing loud and clear,
While the old cat just won't come near.
A dance off starts, it's quite a sight,
With moves that seem both wrong and right.

A monkey's throwing fruit with glee,
While birds look on sarcastically.
They squawk and laugh in joyous jest,
Who knew such chaos could be best?

Beneath the emerald glow so sweet,
Nature's comedy can't be beat.
With each slip and every fall,
It's the laughter that unites us all.

Harmony in the Blossoms' Embrace

In a garden, giggles bloom,
As bees do cha-cha in their room.
The flowers sway with grace and cheer,
While ants perform a march so dear.

A tulip teases a daisy bright,
"You bloom at dawn, but I shine at night!"
The roses blush, a bit perplexed,
As butterflies are quite complexed.

A gopher pops up for a peek,
"What's all this fuss? I'm here for a snack!"
The petals shrink with every joke,
And giggles float like fragrant smoke.

In this embrace of color so bold,
Nature tells stories, fun and untold.
With laughter shared among the leaves,
A symphony that no one grieves.

Rivals of the Serene Horizon

Two frogs perched on a lily pad,
Counting the flies that made them mad.
Each leap a boast, a sly debate,
But who gets the dish—oh, what a fate!

A turtle creeps by—oh so slow,
Laughing at the froggies' show.
"Speed isn't key," he takes a stand,
"Patience is what makes land so grand!"

The wind now joins with a giggling tune,
As clouds drift by, like a laughing loon.
The frogs jump high, but fall on their rear,
Creating a splash that brings hearty cheer.

Rivals they are, in playful tease,
Nature's jesters, with such great ease.
With each croak and whimper, they laugh along,
In this horizon, where all belong.

Embracing the Dappled Sunlight

In sunlight's dance, a lizard pranks,
Chasing shadows and missing its thanks.
A stumble here and a wiggle there,
Makes sunshine giggle, from everywhere.

A hedgehog rolls, with quills so bright,
"I'm just a ball, isn't this right?"
While butterflies plot a crazy flight,
In the warming glow, they feel just right.

A breeze arrives, with whispers bold,
Telling tales of warmth and cold.
As critters join in a sappy rhyme,
Nature plays tricks, oh, what a crime!

Embracing all, with a cheeky wink,
Each moment flows like a joyful drink.
In sunlight's laughter, we find our cue,
To chase the day, and start anew.

Sundrenched Reverie in Bloom

The sun wore its hat, a bright yellow dome,
While ants held a parade, in a chocolate foam.
A monkey on stilts danced, quite a sight,
Yelling, "Get on my level! It's a glorious night!"

With flowers all giggling, they tickled the breeze,
A cactus told jokes, with hilarious ease.
Bumblebees buzzed, set the mood for delight,
While frogs croaked the tunes, singing tales of their plight.

Daisies turned daisies, in the name of romance,
Whilst slugs held a soapbox, declaring a chance.
Their slimy philosophies made others just laugh,
As daisies rolled eyes, sipping dew from a staff.

Laughter cascaded, like rain from the trees,
Where grasshoppers played swing and sway in the breeze.

This world turned comedic, a show without end,
In our floral escapade, where joys never bend.

The Allure of Untamed Eden

A parrot in sneakers strutted with flair,
While zebras played poker, not a worry or care.
Chasing wild chimeras with glittery tails,
Every creature conspired, in laughter it sails.

With fruit, oh so plush, like candy on trees,
A lion in sunglasses yelled, "Share a bite, please!"
While turtles gossip, oh what juicy affairs,
Whispering secrets, beneath leafy wares.

The iguanas threw parties, they danced on the vine,
While lizards all gathered for a slice of divine.
Sloths offered their wisdom, slow but so grand,
"Life's not just a race, get out and take a stand!"

In this wacky wild kingdom, the fun never stops,
Where everyone's laughing, from branches to hops.
Each chuckle and giggle, like birds on the wing,
In this dazzling chaos, who will be king?

Whispers of the Eternal Oasis

A camel in shades, lounging under the sun,
Declared, "This is life, who needs all that run?"
With palm trees debating, confused over shade,
While the wind cracked a smile, its back to the trade.

The puddles were pools, for frogs fit for fun,
Cannonballs made splashes, oh weren't they the ones?
A toucan with style, strutted feathers with pride,
Claimed he was the star of this wild, funny ride.

The sand danced around, in a twist and a twirl,
Cactus confetti made the party unfurl.
As the sun turned to orange, it winked with a cheer,
This lively oasis, where laughter is dear.

What a sight to behold, nature's grand show,
With squirrels delighting, in ruffles of snow.
Each giggle a wave, in a giggling spree,
In our timeless oasis, forever carefree.

Echoes Beneath the Canopy

Beneath leafy giants, where shadows play tricks,
A raccoon in pajamas, doing wild fix.
With squirrels as bandits, they plotted the score,
While the woodpecker drummed, like an old rock encore.

The butterflies giggled, in colors so bright,
As they twirled with the flowers, a whimsical sight.
A rabbit on rollerblades zoomed by the trees,
"Catch me if you can," said with frolicsome glee!

The figs held a meeting, quite juicy, you know,
To discuss all the ways to steal the show.
As the sun played peek-a-boo, from sky to the ground,
This mischief beneath, turned the serious round.

So here in this forest, where laughter is found,
Each echo of joy, like a soft magic sound.
In the laughter of critters, the trees lean in close,
Celebrating the jungle, in delightful prose.

Wanderlust Through Verdant Valleys

In fields where rubber chickens roam,
And flowers wear hats made of foam,
A squirrel juggles acorns with glee,
While bees hum tunes like it's TV.

The rivers run wild with chocolate milk,
And clouds are fluffier than silk.
A bicycle made of jellybeans,
Sails through the air, the craziest scene.

Around the bend, a llama sings,
Wearing a cape and golden rings.
Join the parade of quirky sights,
Under the canopy of delight.

So take a step on this merry trail,
With laughter echoing like a sail.
Explore the paths where silliness waits,
In valleys where joy facilitates.

A Retreat for the Heart and Soul

A hammock sways under a sunny grin,
Where marshmallows dance and giggle, let's begin.
The lemonade flows like a waterfall,
And frogs in tuxedos are having a ball.

Yoga with cats, they nap through the poses,
While daisies chat with the shy pink roses.
Churros float by on clouds of cream,
And laughter bubbles like a joyful stream.

Sipping tea brewed with whimsy and cheer,
With bunnies who whisper, 'no worries here!'
It's a place to recharge, with humor on hold,
In the warmth of a space where silliness unfolds.

So gather your friends for this cute little break,
With fudge-filled piñatas, make no mistake.
Here all the worries slip quietly away,
In a retreat where nonsense rules the day.

Celestial Mornings of Tranquility

The sun yawns wide, wearing yellow pajamas,
While pancakes flip, dodging their dramas.
Comets race through syrupy skies,
And stars do cartwheels in bright surprise.

Birds in bow ties sing songs of delight,
As croissants round up for a morning fright.
The coffee brews with a bubbly cheer,
While squirrels debate the best career.

Clouds gossip over the sweetest breeze,
With hints of cupcake and jelly with ease.
In this whimsical space, day starts with a grin,
A world where pure fun is destined to win.

So rise with a chuckle, let laughter abound,
In mornings where humor knows no bounds.
Sip in the joy, let your worries take flight,
In a cosmos of magic and pure delight.

The Resilient Echo of Growth

In gardens where plants wear glasses and hats,
Cucumbers lounge while plotting with bats.
A sunflower twirls like a fancy dancer,
While tomatoes grumble, 'Who needs an enhancer?'

The roots have a meeting to settle the score,
On which vegetable wins, who'll grow even more?
With old carrots telling the tales of their youth,
While radishes giggle, quite uncouth.

The daisies dabble in the gossip parade,
As seedlings hatch jokes in the warm, cozy shade.
They poke fun at bugs for their silly small flight,
While laughing out loud through the starry night.

So here we find life blooming with quirk,
Through trials and triumphs of every perk.
In a world where the earth knows how to jest,
The echo of growth will always be blessed.

Fables of Winding Rivers

In a land where ducks wear hats,
A frog holds court with chitchat.
He croaks of tides and silly dreams,
While fish swim by in sunlit beams.

A turtle struts on woody docks,
Decked in shades, he surely rocks.
He tells the tale of a lost shoe,
Claiming it smelled like last night's stew.

Otters dance through liquid lanes,
While gophers play their nifty games.
A beaver builds with such great flair,
His dam transformed to a retro fair!

By the bends, the whispers flow,
Of wise old owls who steal the show.
As laughter spills from stream to shore,
Each ripple tells a fable more.

A Vow Beneath the Starlit Canopy

Beneath the twinkling stars so bright,
A raccoon swears he'll never bite.
With berry juice upon his face,
He vows to keep his furry grace.

A squirrel shimmies up a tree,
Proclaiming, "You must dance with me!"
His partner slips on acorn caps,
And soon they both collapse in laps.

The moonlight casts a silver glow,
As bats swing low while snails move slow.
A firefly buzzes, sharing winks,
Creating chaos, oh what kinks!

As owls hoot a sleepy tune,
A hedgehog rolls 'neath the bright moon.
Together as they giggle here,
Their vows are sweet with silly cheer.

Echoes of the Untamed Wild

In jungles where the monkeys swing,
A parrot paints with buzzing bling.
While leopards prance in mismatched socks,
The jungle's void of boring clocks.

A lion roars to welcome joy,
And claims his mane's a special toy.
The zebras laugh, their stripes all askew,
"You really think that's fashion, too?"

Beneath the trees, the creatures prance,
In this wild world, there's no last chance.
A sloth just hangs, refusing fate,
Declaring, "I just can't participate!"

With echoes loud of playful cheer,
The wild remembers to draw near.
In every laugh and silly roar,
The untamed breeze will always soar.

Gossamer Threads of Existence

In gardens where the spiders weave,
A web of dreams that won't deceive.
A butterfly flits, deciding fate,
While ants debate on what's their plate.

A dandelion, with wishes bold,
Whispers secrets of stories told.
While ladybugs march in a row,
They argue which way they should go.

The sunbeams dance on gossamer strands,
As fireflies glow with shining hands.
A bumblebee buzzes, full of cheer,
Mixing nectar with sweet dreams here.

With each tiny thread, a tale is spun,
In the garden where laughter runs.
Life unfolds in whimsical waves,
Creating joy that nature braves.

Requiem for Forgotten Gardens

The daisies once danced, oh so bright,
Now they're just weeds, much to their fright.
The roses complained, 'Where's our parade?'
'Just over there,' said the trees, 'in the shade.'

The gnomes in their stillness break into song,
While the herbs play poker, it won't take long.
The basil's a bluffer, the thyme's quite sly,
In this garden of chaos, they aim for the sky.

The sunflowers argue, who's tallest this year?
The marigolds mutter, 'They're full of hot air.'
But the worms in the soil roll their eyes with glee,
'We've seen all the shows; time for a tea spree.'

So here's to the chaos in the overgrown lot,
Where laughter is louder than the weeds we forgot.
Raise your spade high, be it shovel or hoe,
In this garden of silence, the fun will still grow.

Legends in the Lushness

In jungles so thick, where the parrot does squawk,
Lies a tale of a squirrel who learned how to walk.
He bumbled and fumbled, yet dazzled the crew,
While the owls just hooted, 'Now what will he do?'

The lizards play poker while sunbathing free,
They deal with a swagger, oh, look at that spree!
An iguana bets cheekily, 'I'll raise you a bug!'
And the frogs in the pond just wrap up in a hug.

Every vine whispers secrets of yore,
Of monkeys in tuxes and hippos that snore.
The trees throw a party, with leaves in a swirl,
Where the bashful old tortoise gives twirls like a girl.

Legends get wilder with each passing season,
Transforming the mundane into sweet comic reason.
So if you should wander through this lively scene,
You might leave with giggles and a splash of green.

Memories in the Moment's Glow

Amidst the warm glow of the twilight's sweet haze,
A raccoon holds court in a flashback gaze.
With stories of snacks from the unsuspecting,
While the fireflies flicker, oh, so connecting.

A hedgehog with charm leads the dance on a log,
While the chubby old badger tells tales of their bog.
The shadows all waltz with a soft, silly glee,
As night settles in, and they sip herbal tea.

The moon whispers softly, 'Let's play hide and seek,'
While the bushes all rustle and giggles peek.
The laughter erupts, oh such joyous delight,
In moments of glow that brightened the night.

Every creature delights in the thing called "today,"
Collecting the memories that drifted away.
With a wink and a hop, let the fun flow like streams,
In this earthly kingdom where all share their dreams.

Adventures in Sunbeam Valleys

Through valleys of sunbeams, wild and absurd,
Bumblebees argue — they're quite undeterred.
Each flower wears sunshine like a crown on its head,
And the daisies get jealous of the tulips in red.

The ants pull a prank with a leaf on a hill,
While the dandelions blow fluff, oh what a thrill!
The rabbits hold meetings, discussing their carrots,
And the frogs jump for joy, frees from all their burdens.

A picnic of laughter spreads wide across grass,
As squirrels conduct orchestras, quite the fine class.
With cookie crumbs making their sweet little trails,
Echoes of joy float through these sunbeamy gales.

In adventuring moments where giggles collide,
Every critter rejoices; there's nowhere to hide.
So come join the fray; let your worries disperse,
In sunbeam valleys, let laughter immerse!

Dappled Shadows and Morning Dew

Beneath the trees, the squirrels prance,
Chasing shadows, a comical dance.
A droplet falls, bounces with glee,
Is that a raindrop or just a bee?

The sunlight giggles, peeking through,
As grasshoppers plot their biggest zoo.
A chatty robin, with a tune so bold,
Turns gossip 'gainst the flowers, I'm told.

A slide down the hill - oh what a blunder,
He lands in a puddle, just like thunder.
"Oops!" he chirps, all socks now a soak,
Nature's laughter, as big as a joke.

So here we sit in the dappled light,
Finding joy in each silly sight.
With morning dew as our tickled friend,
May the laughter and fun never end!

Whispers of the Leafy Realm

The leaves are talking, can you hear?
They gossip loudly, quite sincere.
A clumsy beetle bumps on by,
With rumors spreading, oh my, oh my!

The trees, they chuckle, shake with glee,
"Best watch your step, or you'll end up in tea!"
A dandy dandelion, proud as can be,
Plans a parade for all to see.

Oh look! A snail in a top hat, you say?
He's got fine taste in a comical way.
"Bumping along on my grand little path,
Why hurry, dear friends? Let's all have a laugh!"

The whispers rise up to the sky,
Laughing at clouds drifting by.
A kingdom of giggles, wrapping us tight,
In leafy laughter, pure delight.

The Sweet Surrender of Stillness

In the quiet, critters play,
With a napping bear, snoring away.
A tumbleweed does a clumsy roll,
While the frogs throw a splash party – what a shoal!

A pair of ants in a race so bold,
One's stuck in syrup, the other just rolled.
"Quick!" says the one, "We've no time to waste,
There's a picnic ahead – get ready to taste!"

A chipmunk giggles, munching on snacks,
As the butterfly flutters, daring to crack.
"Watch it now!" yells a bush, trees start to sway,
"Dare we disturb this fine lazy day?"

As jesters all, in this calm retreat,
The stillness dances to a fumble beat.
With nature laughing at the silly sights,
In this quiet, all makes merry delights.

Nature's Kiss at Daybreak

The sun peeks through with a warm embrace,
Waking up flowers in a sleepy race.
A hedgehog yawns, then tumbles about,
"Not ready yet, please, I just want to pout!"

The daisies giggle, their petals afluff,
As gentle breezes tease, just enough.
A butterfly lands with a wink and a grin,
"Let's dance for joy, let the fun begin!"

The morning's chatter fills the air,
A chicken clucks, "There's oats over there!"
While cats stretch wide at the break of dawn,
Planning mischief before they yawn.

So raise your cups of good cheer and glee,
For nature's fun is as grand as can be.
In this fresh start, we let laughter swing,
With a kiss so light, let the joy take wing!

Songbirds of the Glittering Vale

Songbirds chirp with tales to tell,
Of a snail who danced at a wishing well.
Their feathers bright, they flutter and flit,
Winging through skies, where laughter is lit.

A parrot named Lou, quite the prankster,
Swapped his song for a crazy canister.
With honks and quacks, he stole the show,
Making all critters laugh, "Oh no, oh no!"

Under the sun, they joke and sing,
Chasing each other, a comical fling.
A dance-off begins, oh what a sight,
While rabbits and foxes join in delight.

In the vale where giggles play,
Nature's humor leads the way.
With every tweet and every croon,
Life feels like a silly cartoon.

Where Gentle Breezes Linger

Where gentle breezes softly prance,
A squirrel donned a bright pink dance.
His acorn hat askew on his head,
He twirled and spun, nearly fled.

The wind whispered secrets, quite absurd,
Of a wise old owl who just loved to word.
He told jokes to the trees, they laughed in glee,
"Who cooks for you?" he hooted, oh me!

Bunnies bounced around in bright bow ties,
While dandelions shared humorous lies.
"The sun's our DJ," the flowers all said,
As shadows began to dance 'round their bed.

In this quirky realm of breeze-filled cheer,
Every day brings mirth so near.
With each gust, a chuckle springs,
Nature's laughter, the joy it brings.

Macaws and Moonbeams

Macaws soared high in the moon's soft light,
Squawking of snacks in the starry night.
One claimed to see a jellybean tree,
And danced through the air, wild and free.

Under the stars, a party began,
With moonbeams and fruit-flavored cans.
Parrots juggled coconuts, quite the feat,
While crabs on the beach joined in the beat.

As the night wore on, the fun never ceased,
Chasing reflections, the laughter released.
They played hide-and-seek with a starfish they found,
While ocean waves provided the sound.

In this vibrant scene of feathered delight,
The world felt like a whimsical fright.
With every hoot and every cheer,
The macaws kept the joy flowing near.

The Calm of Shimmering Waters

The calm of waters, all glimmering bright,
A fish wore a hat, oh what a sight!
With flip-flops on fins, he strolled with flair,
As turtles giggled, "Is that real hair?"

A frog in a boat, with snacks piled high,
Paddled in circles, he couldn't deny.
"Came for a swim, stayed for the cake!"
With ripples of laughter, the pond gave a shake.

Dragonflies danced, in silly parade,
Spinning and twirling, a headache they made.
"Who's leading this mess?" the herons would scoff,
Yet bright little creatures would never scoff off.

In waters that shimmer, and thoughts full of cheer,
Every splash brought a chuckle near.
With every ripple, a story ensued,
In a land where laughter and joy have brewed.

Love Letters Written in Blossoms

Roses write notes, what a scene,
Tulips giggle and turn bright green.
Daisies whisper secrets on the breeze,
While violets chuckle, oh what a tease!

Petals flutter, like little wings,
Sending messages of silly things.
Sunshine tickles the thorns just right,
As flowers dance in pure delight.

Bees join in with buzzing cheers,
As blooms laugh away their fears.
A bouquet of jest in every hue,
Love letters bloom, both bold and true!

With each stem, a tale unfolds,
In garden corners, laughter molds.
Nature's comedy, oh so bright,
Making our hearts take flight tonight!

Underneath the Velvet Skies

Stars tell jokes from way up high,
While comets wink and sigh.
Moonlight slips on a banana peel,
As twilight's giggles softly heal.

A breeze with a tickle, oh so fun,
Whispers nonsense to everyone.
Clouds making faces, puffed all around,
In this scene, joy is found!

Fireflies catch laughter in their glow,
Creating magic in the flow.
Even the night makes silly sounds,
As the world spins on with merry bounds!

Beneath this velvet, playful dome,
Everything feels like a silly poem.
No worries here, just nighttime glee,
As if the stars are wild and free!

Vistas of Laughing Waterfalls

Cascading giggles through the trees,
Splashes of joy on gentle knees.
Water dances with a playful tune,
Singing to the sun and moon.

Pebbles join in, skipping along,
For every ripple sings a song.
Fish flip and flop in pure ballet,
Under the sun's warm, golden ray!

Moss smiles with a cushy grin,
As lilies party, let the fun begin!
With every splash, a chuckle grows,
Nature's laughter flows and flows.

Bubbling streams of silly cheer,
Make each moment bright and clear.
In this joyous, frothy spree,
Even rocks rustle with glee!

Treasures of the Verdant Realm

In green fields where giggles bloom,
Dandelions dance, dispelling gloom.
Grasshoppers prance with leaps of joy,
Each jump's a laugh, oh what a ploy!

Trees whisper secrets, tickling each leaf,
As shadows play games, like a thief.
Acorns roll with a clumsy cheer,
While squirrels laugh, "The coast is clear!"

In this treasure trove of silliness,
Nature's quirks are a true finesse.
Blooming with fun in each design,
Every petal has a punchline!

With sunshine painting the day so bright,
There's no room for worries in this light.
Let's gather the joy and put on a show,
In the verdant realm where laughter flows!

The Lush Embrace of Serenity

Amidst the trees they dance with glee,
Sipping nectar, wild and free.
A parrot squawks, it tells a joke,
While monkeys swing and silly poke.

Laughter echoes through the glade,
As an old turtle joins the parade.
Everyone's wearing silly hats,
Even startled camouflaged spats!

The flowers giggle, petals bright,
Unfurling cheer in morning light.
A frog attempts to croon a tune,
But croaks instead with much buffoon.

So come unwind in this fair bliss,
Where every moment's sealed with a kiss.
In the midst of joy, we find our place,
Lush greenery wraps us in warm embrace.

Veils of Verdant Serenity

The leaves whisper tales so absurd,
Of frogs who dream of becoming bird.
A snail races, claiming it's fast,
But really, it's too slow to last.

Sunbeams sprinkle laughter on the ground,
Where silly shadows dance around.
A gossiping brook shares secrets untold,
Of a dancing lizard, so brave and bold.

The breeze tickles flowers' shy blooms,
While bees boast of their grand perfumes.
A lazy cat lounges with style,
Waking to photogenic smile!

So sit in this mirthful realm today,
Where silliness leads the fun ballet.
Let nature's comedy take the stage,
Forever young, dance with no age.

Fruitful Dawn of Delights

Morning bursts with colors bright,
A pineapple wears a crown—what a sight!
The oranges giggle, lemons pout,
While grapes gossip, flinging doubt.

A squirrel tries to climb a pear,
Tumbles down, no single care.
Bananas peel themselves for fun,
Yelling, "Catch me! I'm on the run!"

Ripe berries burst with juicy tales,
Of mischief-ships on sugary sails.
A watermelon slips in the stream,
Making the others laugh and scream!

Join the party, it's a fruity spree,
With every bite, you're guaranteed glee.
In this garden of joyous sights,
Dawn reveals a harvest of delights.

Tapestry of Colorful Fantasies

A canvas blooms with hues so bright,
Where flowers wear shoes of pure white.
Butterflies toss confetti in air,
While frogs don tuxedos, fine and rare.

In this land where nonsense reigns,
A cow plays chess, and a bird complains.
They sip on dew from golden cups,
Singing songs of fantastical ups.

A rainbow strolls with swagger bold,
Telling tales of adventures bold.
Two kittens wearing bejeweled crowns,
Lead parades through this jesting town.

Let laughter paint your day so bright,
In this whimsical, wild delight.
Surrounded by joy, take this chance,
Join the merry, fanciful dance!

www.ingramcontent.com/pod-product-compliance
Lightning Source LLC
Chambersburg PA
CBHW072119070526
44585CB00016B/1499